Foundational Skills

Phonics
for
second Grade

drum

cake

SHELL EDUCATION

Contributing Authors

Jodene Smith, M.S.

Mary Rosenberg, M.A.Ed.

Suzanne I. Barchers, Ed.D.

Chandra Prough, M.A.Ed.

Christine Dugan, M.A.Ed.

Publishing Credits

Robin Erickson, *Production Director;* Lee Aucoin, *Creative Director;* Timothy J. Bradley, *Illustration Manager*; Sara Johnson, M.S.Ed., *Editorial Director;* Evelyn Garcia, *Editor;* Grace Alba, *Designer*; Corinne Burton, M.A.Ed., *Publisher*

Standards

© 2010 National Governors Association Center for Best Practices and Council of Chief State School Officers (CCSS)

Shell Education

5301 Oceanus Drive

Huntington Beach, CA 92649-1030

http://www.shelleducation.com

ISBN 978-1-4258-1100-6

© 2014 Shell Education Publishing, Inc.

Table of Contents

Developing Foundational Skills in Reading

Foundational Skills: Phonics for Second Grade has been written with second graders in mind! The pages in this book provide children practice with some of the foundational skills needed to be successful readers—phonics and word recognition.

There has been much written and said about phonics. All the talk has left questions about what phonics is and whether it should be taught. Simply put, phonics is the relationship between letters and sounds. When a child learns that the letter *s* makes the /s/ sound, that is phonics! Since children need to be able to figure out words in order to read, it is important that they understand the relationship between the letters that are on the page and the sounds the letters make (Chall 1995).

There has been much research to show that phonics needs to be explicitly taught and included in good reading programs. In fact, the National Reading Panel (2000) included phonics as one of the five essential components of reading instruction. The fact is that a large number of words in English do follow patterns and rules. Instruction and practice with phonics gives children an opportunity to develop their understanding of the relationship between letters and sounds. Additionally, researchers have found that phonic awareness is a strong predictor of later reading achievement (Juel 1988, Griffith and Gough 1986, Lomax and McGee 1987, Tunmer and Nesdale 1985).

But not all words can be figured out with phonics (Cook 2004). For example, the words *of* and *the* cannot be sounded out with knowledge of letter and sound relationships. There are several word lists that have been compiled of words that occur in print with high frequency, and many of these words do not follow patterns and rules (Fry and Kress 2006). Children need to know other ways to read or figure out words that they cannot apply phonics to, such as recognizing words by sight or using context. For this reason, practice with frequently occurring, grade-level-appropriate sight words is an important component of reading.

This book provides children with many opportunities to practice key skills in both phonics and word recognition. Practicing these skills help build the foundation for successful readers. And although the traditional saying is "practice makes perfect," a better saying for this book is "practice makes successful readers."

Understanding the Standards

The Common Core State Standards were developed through the Common Core State Standards Initiative. The standards have been adopted by many states in an effort to create a clear and consistent framework and to prepare students for higher education and the workforce. The standards were developed as educators worked together to incorporate the most effective models from around the country and globe, to provide teachers and parents with a shared understanding of what students are expected to learn at each grade level, and as a continuum throughout the grades. Whereas previously used state-developed standards showed much diversity in what was covered at each grade level, the consistency of the Common Core State Standards provides educators a common understanding of what should be covered at each grade level and to what depth.

The Common Core State Standards have the following qualities:

- They are aligned with college and work expectations.

- They are clear, understandable, and consistent.

- They include rigorous content and application of knowledge through high-order skills.

- They build upon strengths and lessons of current state standards.

- They are informed by other top-performing countries so that all students are prepared to succeed in our global economy and society.

- They are evidence based.

Students who meet these standards within their K–12 educations should have the skills and knowledge necessary to succeed in their educational careers and beyond.

Getting Started

Practicing the phonics skills targeted in this book gives children the foundation they need to become better readers. It is because you realize this that you have purchased this book! Following are some tips for using this book:

- Set aside a specific time of day to work on the activities found in this book. This will establish consistency.

- Emphasize completing a couple of pages each time the child works in the book rather than lots of activity pages at one time.

- Keep all practice sessions positive and constructive. If the mood becomes tense or you and the child get frustrated, set the activities aside and look for another time for the child to practice.

- Help with instructions, if necessary. If the child is having difficulty understanding what to do, talk through some of the problems with him or her.

- Use the answer key provided on pages 87–93. Once the desired number of pages have been completed, help check the work. If possible, take time to go back and correct any problems missed. Immediately reviewing errors with the help of an adult helps children learn from their mistakes.

Making It Work

Understanding the key features of this book will help you effectively use this book as you work with the child to develop and practice reading skills. Following are some features of the book that will help you.

- **Standards-based practice.** The exercises in *Foundational Skills: Phonics for Second Grade* are aligned with the Common Core State Standards. Each activity page focuses on a particular concept, skill, or skill set and provides students opportunities to practice and achieve mastery.

- **Clear, easy-to-understand activities**. The exercises in this book are written in a user-friendly style.

- **Stand-alone activity pages.** Each activity is flexible and can be used independently.

- **Concise number of exercises.** The number of exercises on each page is limited to six. Children feel more comfortable and confident in attempting a page when the number of exercises is not overwhelming to them.

The chart below provides suggestions for how to implement the activities.

Preteaching	Reteaching
Choose pages with concepts the child has not yet learned. This will take some teaching on your part in order to help the child understand the concept, so be sure you are comfortable and prepared to explain the new concept.	Use pages related to concepts the child has struggled with in school or while doing homework. If there are any areas or specific standards with which the child may need some additional instruction and practice, use the Standards Correlation Chart on page 9 to help locate pages that will be useful.
Practice	**Review**
Select pages that are consistent with what is being taught in school. By providing additional practice with those reading concepts, you will help the child master them more quickly.	Choose pages with concepts the child may have learned earlier in the school year. By reviewing previously taught concepts, the child will benefit from refreshing those skills.

Correlations to Standards

Shell Education is committed to producing educational materials that are research- and standards-based. In this effort, we have correlated all of our products to the academic standards of all 50 United States, the District of Columbia, the Department of Defense Dependent Schools, and all Canadian provinces. We have also correlated to the Common Core State Standards.

How to Find Standards Correlations

To print a customized correlation report of this product for your state, visit our website at **http://www.shelleducation.com** and follow the on-screen directions. If you require assistance in printing correlation reports, please contact Customer Service at 1-877-777-3450.

Purpose and Intent of Standards

Legislation mandates that all states adopt academic standards that identify the skills students will learn in kindergarten through grade twelve. Many states also have standards for pre-K. This same legislation sets requirements to ensure the standards are detailed and comprehensive.

Standards are designed to focus instruction and guide adoption of curricula. Standards are statements that describe the criteria necessary for students to meet specific academic goals. They define the knowledge, skills, and content students should acquire at each level. Standards are also used to develop standardized tests to evaluate students' academic progress. Teachers are required to demonstrate how their lessons meet state standards. State standards are used in the development of all of our products, so educators can be assured they meet the academic requirements of each state.

Common Core State Standards

The lessons in this book are aligned to the Common Core State Standards (CCSS). The standards listed on page 9 support the objectives presented throughout the lessons.

Correlations to Standards

Skill	Pages
Distinguish long and short vowels when reading regularly spelled one-syllable words.	11–25
Know spelling-sound correspondences for additional common vowel teams.	26–41
Decode regularly spelled two-syllable words with long vowels.	46–47
Read words with inflectional endings.	42–45
Use knowledge of the meaning of individual words to predict the meaning of compound words.	48–51
Decode words with common prefixes and suffixes.	52–63
Identify words with inconsistent but common spelling-sound correspondences.	64–73
Recognize and read grade-appropriate irregularly spelled words.	74–85

Letter Formation Guide

Long and Short Vowel Words

Name: _____ **Date:** _____

Directions: Name each picture. Circle the vowel sound you hear.

1.  a e i o u	2.  a e i o u
3.  a e i o u	4.  a e i o u
5. 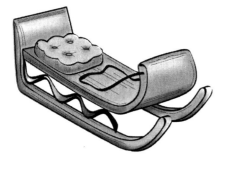 a e i o u	6.  a e i o u

Long and Short Vowel Words

Name: _____**Date:** _____

Directions: Name each picture. Circle the vowel sound you hear.

1.  a e i o u	2. 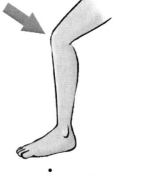 a e i o u
3.  a e i o u	4.  a e i o u
5.  a e i o u	6.  a e i o u

Long and Short Vowel Words

Name: _____ **Date:** _____

Directions: Name each picture. Fill in the bubble to show if the vowel sound is long or short.

1. ◯ short ◯ long

2. ◯ short ◯ long

3. ◯ short ◯ long

4. ◯ short ◯ long

5. ◯ short ◯ long

6. ◯ short ◯ long

Long and Short *a*

Name: _____ **Date:** _____

Directions: Name each picture. Write the word on the line.

Word Bank

crab	square	hand
game	cake	cat

1.

_____

2.

_____

3.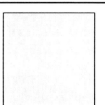

_____

4.

_____

5.

_____

6.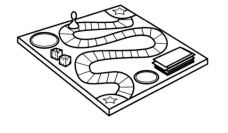

_____

Long and Short *e*

Name: _____ **Date:** _____

Directions: Draw a line from each word to the picture.

1. sled

2. seal

3. tent

4. peas

5. nest

6. belt

Long and Short *i*

Name: _____ **Date:** _____

Directions: Circle the word that names the picture.

1.  crib cribe	2.  nin nine
3.  ring rige	4.  stick sticke
5.  mick mice	6.  bik bike

Name: _____ **Date:** _____

Directions: Draw a picture of each word. Then write if the vowel sound is *long* or *short*.

1. bone	2. globe
_____	_____
3. frog	4. doll
_____	_____
5. stone	6. pond
_____	_____

Long and Short *u*

Name: _____ **Date:** _____

Directions: Read the clues. Write the correct word and if the vowel sound is long or short

Word Bank

~~skunk~~	June	lunch
duck	mule	sun

1. it stinks

    <u>skunk</u>

    ● short ○ long

2. it quacks

    _____

    ○ short ○ long

3. a month

    _____

    ○ short ○ long

4. you eat it

    _____

    ○ short ○ long

5. it kicks

    _____

    ○ short ○ long

6. it shines

    _____

    ○ short ○ long

Long and Short Vowel Mixed Review

Name: _____ **Date:** _____

Directions: Name each picture. Write the correct word and if the vowel sound is long or short.

Word Bank

rake   tree   ~~vest~~

truck   lock   vine

1. ● short ○ long

vest
_____

2. ○ short ○ long

_____

3. ○ short ○ long

_____

4. ○ short ○ long

_____

5. ○ short ○ long

_____

6. ○ short ○ long

_____

Long and Short Vowel Mixed Review

Name: _____ **Date:** _____

Directions: Read each sentence. Circle *yes* or *no* if it could happen.

1. A whale has a vest.  yes no	2. A queen quacks.  yes no
3. A pup skates.  yes no	4. A kid can bike.  yes no
5. A fish gets dice. 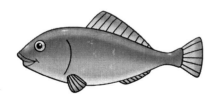 yes no	6. A fire is cold.  yes no

Long Vowel Mixed Review

Name: _____ **Date:** _____

Directions: Add an *e* to the end of each word. Draw a line from the word to the correct picture.

1. cap___

2. pin___

3. dim___

4. tap___

5. can___

Long and Short Vowel Mixed Review

Name: _____ **Date:** _____

Directions: Name each picture. Complete the crossword puzzle.

Word Bank

kit   tap   tail   ear   kite   tape

Across

1

2

3

Down

2

5

4

Long and Short Vowel Mixed Review

Name: _____ **Date:** _____

Directions: Circle the best word to complete each sentence. Write the word on the line.

1. He used a _____ to clean the floor.	mop mope
2. He broke his _____ .	tow toe
3. A _____ is in the vase.	ross rose
4. The bunny will _____ back home.	hope hop
5. When it is cold, wear a _____ .	cot coat

Long and Short Vowel Mixed Review

Name: _____ **Date:** _____

Directions: Practice reading each sentence. Then draw a picture for each sentence.

1. A dog has nine plums for lunch.	2. The frog can sleep in a bed.
3. The duck is in a hole.	4. A crab has dice.
5. A whale is pink.	6. The bee rides in a cab.

Long and Short Vowel Mixed Review

Name: _____ **Date:** _____

Directions: Write the words in the correct column.

Word Bank

made   hunt   rob   spine   hope
steel   black   twig

Short Vowel	Long Vowel
_____	_____
_____	_____
_____	_____
_____	_____

Long *a* Spelling Patterns

Name: _____ **Date:** _____

Directions: Write the answer to each riddle. Use the spelling hint for help.

Word Bank

race	mail	sail
stare	tale	case

Riddle	Spelling Hint	Answer
1. You do this to a letter.	nail	
2. to look at another person for a long time	square	
3. A boat can have one.	tail	
4. You can win this.	face	
5. a story	whale	
6. A detective has this.	vase	

Long e Spelling Patterns

Name: _____ **Date:** _____

Directions: Draw lines to match the words and pictures. Then sort the words by their spelling patterns.

seal		read	
bee		sunny	
bunny		weep	
money		queen	
beak		honey	
feet		beach	

-ee Spelling Pattern	-ea Spelling Pattern	-y Spelling Pattern
_____	_____	_____
_____	_____	_____
_____	_____	_____
_____	_____	_____

Long *i* Spelling Patterns

Name: _____ **Date:** _____

Directions: Sort each word by the long *i* spelling pattern. Write the word that names the picture.

Word Bank

cry	pie	mice	sky
bike	tie	five	fly

i-e	-ie	-y
_____	_____	_____
5		
_____	_____	_____
_____		_____

Name: _____ **Date:** _____

Directions: Solve the riddles with words from the Word Bank. Circle the letters that make the long *o* vowel sound.

Word Bank

coat   rose   gold   toe   bow   ~~crow~~

1. It is a kind of bird.

   _____

2. It is a kind of flower.

   _____

3. It is a color.

   _____

4. You tie this around a gift.

   _____

5. You wear it.

   _____

6. It is on your foot.

   _____

Long *u* Spelling Patterns

Name: _____ **Date:** _____

Directions: Name each picture. Write the correct word. Circle the letters that make the long *u* sound.

Word Bank

fruit   cube   flute   tube   mule   June

1.  _____	2.  _____
3.  _____	4. 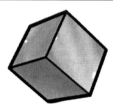 _____
5.  _____	6.  _____

Common Vowel Team Rhymes

Name: _____ **Date:** _____

Directions: Write a word that rhymes with the picture shown. Use the words from the Word Bank.

Word Bank
road   tail   pie   mow   try   suit

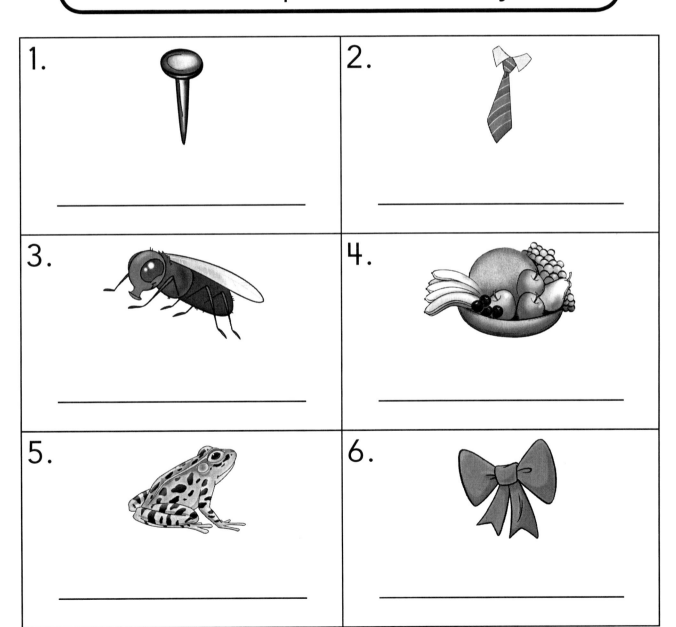

1. _____

2. _____

3. _____

4. _____

5. _____

6. _____

Common Vowel Team Rhymes

Name: _____ **Date:** _____

Directions: Write a word that rhymes with the underlined word. Use the words from the Word Bank.

Word Bank

seal   cake   mile   fruit   more

1. I hope dad will not <u>snore</u> any _____.

2. The man in a <u>suit</u> is eating _____.

3. She ran a _____ with a <u>smile</u>.

4. Tim can <u>bake</u> a _____.

5. The _____ is having a <u>meal</u>.

Name: _____ **Date:** _____

Directions: Draw a line from the word to the correct picture.

1. book

2. wood

3. stood

4. cook

5. hook

6. hood

Vowel Team -oo

Name: _____ **Date:** _____

Directions: Read the sentences. Write the word from the Word Bank that is the best answer.

Word Bank

pool   school   moo
hoop   food

1. It is a place you go to learn. What is it?	_____
2. You can swim in it. What is it?	_____
3. You eat it. What is it?	_____
4. It is what a cow says. What is it?	_____
5. You try to put a basketball in it. What is it?	_____

Vowel Teams -*ou* and -*ow*

Name: _____ **Date:** _____

Directions: Underline the -*ou* and -*ow* words in each sentence. Then draw each picture.

1. Draw a mouse and a cow.	2. Draw a round snout on a pig.
3. Draw a brown hound.	4. Draw a town with 5 houses.
5. Draw a clown with funny eyebrows.	6. Draw a ten-pound trout.

Vowel Team -*aw*

Name: _____**Date:** _____

Directions: Draw a line to match each clue with the best word.

1. the foot of a dog   straw

2. you use it to drink   paw

3. the sound of a crow   caw

4. a baby deer   claw

5. the nail of a lion   fawn

6. a tool   saw

Vowel Team -*ar*

Name: _____ **Date:** _____

Directions: Name each picture. Write the correct word from the Word Bank.

Word Bank

party	star	jar
car	harp	shark	barn

3-Letter Words		_____ _____
4-Letter Words		_____ _____
5-Letter Words		_____ _____

Vowel Teams -er, -ir, and -ur

Name: _____ **Date:** _____

Directions: Draw a picture of each word. Circle the letters that make the /er/ sound.

-er	her	herd
-ir	bird	shirt
-ur	nurse	purse

Name: _____ **Date:** _____

Directions: Change letters in each word to make new words.

Start with
cord

1.

Change the
D to an N   _____

2.

Change the
C to an H   _____

3.

Change the
H to a T   _____

4.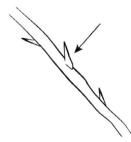

Add an
H after the
T   _____

Mixed Vowel Teams Practice

Name: _____ **Date:** _____

Directions: Circle the two words in each row that have the same vowel sound.

1. (year)   (seed)   bed

2. by   tin   fine

3. book   tool   cook

4. now   crow   snow

5. star   bat   bar

6. boy   song   join

Mixed Vowel Teams Practice

Name: _____ **Date:** _____

Directions: Circle the word that best completes the sentence. Write the word on the line.

1. Pick up your food with a _____.	fort (fork) for
2. My teacher put a _____ on my paper.	tar sad star
3. Dad can _____ a person well.	raw saw draw
4. Don't _____ your hand on the stove.	burn bun bird
5. My mother will _____ for the party.	book food cook
6. Hearing the harp fills me with _____.	boy joy join

Inflectional Ending -*er*

Name: _____ **Date:** _____

Directions: Add -*er* to the words in the second column. Write the complete words in the third column.

Clue	Add -*er*	Complete Word
1. one who teaches	teach _er_	_teacher_
2. one who paints	paint____	_____
3. one who sleeps	sleep____	_____
4. one who dreams	dream____	_____
5. one who cleans	clean____	_____
6. one who trains	train____	_____

Name: _____ **Date:** _____

Directions: Add *-ing* to each word below. Write the word in the puzzle.

Across

1 spray ___ing___
2 pray _____
3 steam _____

Down

1 stain _____
3 soak _____
4 nest _____

Inflectional Ending -ed

Name: _____ **Date:** _____

Directions: Add –ed to each word. Write it in the sentence.

1. heat_ed_	She ___heated___ the food.
2. boast___	My sister _____ about her report card.
3. wait___	Mom _____ for me to finish.
4. coast___	We _____ along the sidewalk on the skateboard.
5. greet___	Tom _____ the visitors.

Inflectional Endings -*ing* and -*ed*

Name: _____ **Date:** _____

Directions: Add –*ing* and –*ed* to each word. Then practice reading the words.

	-*ing*	-*ed*
1. play	playing	played
2. need		
3. paint		
4. float		
5. scream		
6. mail		

Two-Syllable Long Vowel Words

Name: _____ **Date:** _____

Directions: Draw lines to match the words and pictures. Then practice reading the words.

1. bacon

2. table

3. zero

4. soda

5. fever

6. paper

Two-Syllable Long Vowel Words

Name: _____ **Date:** _____

Directions: Write the word for each animal on the line. Then practice reading the words.

Word Bank

spider	zebra	eagle
beetle	beaver	~~tiger~~

1. tiger _____

2. _____

3. _____

4. _____

5. _____

6. _____

Compound Words

Name: _____ **Date:** _____

Directions: Write a compound word to match each picture. Then practice reading the compound words.

Word Bank

~~man~~   air   bow   box   tea   shell

mail   rain   sea   plane   ~~fire~~   cup

1.   fireman _____

2.    _____

3.   _____

4.   _____

5.    _____

6.    _____

Name: _____ **Date:** _____

Directions: Read the compound words. Divide each compound word into its two parts.

1. snowflake = _snow_ + _flake_

2. sailboat = _____ + _____

3. grapefruit = _____ + _____

4. whiteboard = _____ + _____

5. hairbrush = _____ + _____

6. airplane = _____ + _____

Compound Words

Name: _____ **Date:** _____

Directions: Write each compound word in the correct row.

┌───┐
│   **Word Bank**   │
│   butterfly   ~~grapefruit~~   spaceman   │
│   goldfish   strawberry   fireman   │
└───┘

Fruits	grapefruit _____ _____
Animals	_____ _____
Jobs	_____ _____

Compound Words

Name: _____ **Date:** _____

Directions: Write the compound word that is the answer. Then practice reading the words.

1. A **boat** with a **sail** is a

   _____ sailboat _____.

2. A **ball** made of **snow** is a

   _____.

3. A **plane** that flies in the **air** is an

   _____.

4. A **box** for your **mail** is a

   _____.

5. A **cup** you use for **tea** is a

   _____.

6. The **time** you go to **bed** is your

   _____.

Prefix re-

Name: _____ **Date:** _____

Directions: Circle the prefix re- in each word. Then write the base word.

> re- = to do again

1. (re)check _check_ _____	2. rename _____
3. replay _____	4. rewrite _____
5. redo _____	6. retry _____

Name: _____ **Date:** _____

Directions: Add the prefix *dis-* to each word below. Then draw a line to match each word with the opposite of the word.

> ## *dis-* = the opposite of

1. agree   _**dis**_ appear

2. appear   _____ obey

3. obey   _____ agree

4. like   _____ color

5. color   _____ like

6. able   _____ able

Prefix *over-*

Directions: Add the prefix *over-* to the base words below. Then practice reading the words.

> *over-* = too much

1. grown overgrown	2. cook _____
3. do _____	4. mix _____
5. eat _____	6. study _____

Name: _____ **Date:** _____

Directions: Add *un-* to each base word to make a new word. Write the new word on the line to complete the sentence.

> *un-* = not

1. happy	The dog looks __unhappy__.
2. buckle	_____ the seatbelt when you arrive at home.
3. equal	Three and ten are _____.
4. lock	Dad has to _____ the car doors.
5. tie	Please _____ your shoes before taking them off.

Prefix *pre-*

Name: _____ **Date:** _____

Directions: Add the prefix *pre-* to each base word. Write the word on the line.

> *pre-* = before

1. view   _____preview_____

2. season   _____

3. write   _____

4. made   _____

5. heat   _____

6. mix   _____

Name: _____ **Date:** _____

Directions: Add –*er* and –*est* to each base word. Then practice reading the new words.

> -*er* = more   -*est* = most

	-er	-est
1. fast	faster	fastest
2. smart		
3. deep		
4. rich		
5. slow		
6. tall		

Suffix -er

Name: _____ **Date:** _____

Directions: Name each picture. Add –er to the base word in the Word Bank. Write it on the line.

-er = one who

Word Bank

read   farm   ~~teach~~   paint

1.  teacher	2.  _____
3.  _____	4.  _____

Name: _____ **Date:** _____

Directions: Circle the suffix -*less*. Underline the base word. Then practice reading the words.

-*less* = without

1. <u>tire</u>(less)

2. joyless

3. selfless

4. hopeless

5. ageless

6. boneless

Suffix -*ful*

Name: _____ **Date:** _____

Directions: Add the suffix –*ful* to each base word in bold.

-*ful* = full of

Across
1 full of **thought**_____
2 full of **help**_____

Down
3 full of **fear**_____
4 full of **hope**_____
5 full of **flavor**_____
6 full of **care**_____

Name: _____ **Date:** _____

Directions: Put the base word and the suffix -*ness* together to make a new word. Then practice reading the word.

> -*ness* = state or quality of

1. kind   + ness = __kindness__

2. cold   + ness = _____

3. good + ness = _____

4. dark   + ness = _____

5. clever + ness = _____

6. aware + ness = _____

Suffix -ish

Name: _____ **Date:** _____

Directions: Circle the suffix -ish in each word. Then write the base word and practice reading the new word.

> *-ish* = relating to

1. child(ish)

   child

2. greenish

   _____

3. foolish

   _____

4. newish

   _____

5. selfish

   _____

6. babyish

   _____

Prefix and Suffix Review

Name: _____ Date: _____

Directions: Circle the prefix or suffix in each word. Separate the word into the affix and the base word.

	affix	base
1. (re)write	= __re__	+ __write__
2. overgrown	= _____	+ _____
3. kindness	= _____	+ _____
4. disagree	= _____	+ _____
5. tireless	= _____	+ _____

Homonyms

Name: _____ **Date:** _____

Directions: Match each picture to the word that names it.

bill

duck

watch

bowl

Homonyms

Name: _____ **Date:** _____

Directions: Write the word that matches both pictures.

> ## Word Bank
> ring   ~~bark~~   bat   wave

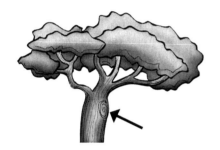 bark

 _____

 _____

 _____

Homonyms

Name: _____ **Date:** _____

Directions: Use each word from the Word Bank two times to complete the sentences.

Word Bank
match   ball   stick

1. Jane got a dress for the ___ball___.

2. The _____ fell down from the tree.

3. Do not play with the _____.

4. I will _____ the papers in my folder.

5. I help mom _____ the socks.

6. Throw the _____ to me!

Homonyms

Name: _____ **Date:** _____

Directions: Write a sentence to show the other meaning of each word.

Word	Sentence—1st Meaning	Your Sentence—2nd Meaning
1. spell	There was a magic spell on the prince.	
2. fan	I am a fan of rock music.	
3. bank	The children played on the bank of the river.	
4. play	I went to see the play Music Man.	

Homophones

Name: _____ Date: _____

Directions: Write a word from the Word Bank that sounds the same as the picture.

Word Bank

would ~~pair~~ plain sent to I

1. pear		2. plane	
pair		_____	
3. eye		4. **2** two	
_____		_____	
5. wood		6. cent	
_____		_____	

1. pear — _pair_

2. plane — _____

3. eye — _____

4. **2** two — _____

5. wood — _____

6. cent — _____

Name: _____ **Date:** _____

Directions: Draw lines to match the sentences and pictures.

1.    There is <u>one</u> pear.

2.    He <u>won</u> the spelling bee.

3. 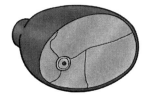   We will cook <u>meat</u> for dinner.

4.    It is nice to shake hands when you <u>meet</u>.

5. 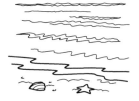   The <u>sea</u> has many waves.

6.    I can <u>see</u> the apples in the tree.

Homophones

Name: _____ **Date:** _____

Directions: Complete each sentence with a word from the Word Bank.

> ## Word Bank
> ~~by~~   for   know   buy   four   No

1. The dog is standing _____by_____ the tree.

2. I _____ how to add.

3. The gift is _____ you.

4. A cat has _____ legs.

5. Mom went to _____ eggs.

6. _____! Do not touch the fire!

Homophones

Name: _____ **Date:** _____

Directions: Circle the name for each picture.

1.  son (sun)	2.  flower flour
3. **8** ate eight	4.  sail sale
5. **2** too two	6.  aunt ant

Homophones

Name: _____ **Date:** _____

Directions: Write each word in the correct space in the sentence.

1.	hear here	Come over _here_ so you can _hear_ me.
2.	be bee	She should not _____ close to the _____ hive.
3.	made maid	The _____ _____ dinner for us.
4.	seam seem	It does not _____ that we can fix the rip in the _____.
5.	tale tail	We read a _____ about a dog who chased his _____.

Homophones

Name: _____ **Date:** _____

Directions: Write a sentence to show the meaning of word 2.

Word 1	Sentence	Word 2	Your Sentence
1. knew	I knew about the surprise.	new	
2. break	She took a break from cleaning.	brake	
3. rowed	Max rowed the boat on the lake.	road	
4. son	His son is six years old.	sun	

Irregularly Spelled Words

Name: _____ **Date:** _____

Directions: Read the words in the Word Box. Write the answers to the riddles on the lines.

> ## Word Bank
>
> one   eight   knew
>
> write   ~~would~~   which

1. sounds like *wood*

   ___would___

2. sounds like *new*

   _____

3. sounds like *right*

   _____

4. sounds like *ate*

   _____

5. sounds like *witch*

   _____

6. sounds like *won*

   _____

Irregularly Spelled Words

Name: _____ **Date:** _____

Directions: Unscramble the word to complete the sentence. Use the Word Bank.

> ## Word Bank
> always   enough   ~~friend~~
> please   school

1. dirfne	Jack is my best friend.
2. eleasp	Can you _____ help me?
3. gnoehu	I have had _____ to eat.
4. olsoch	I get to _____ by bus.
5. wsalay	She is _____ nice to me.

Irregularly Spelled Words

Name: _____ **Date:** _____

Directions: Write the antonym (opposite) of each word from the Word Bank. Fill in the crossword puzzle

Word Bank

high	~~kind~~	night
read	light	group

Across

1 mean _kind_

2 single _____

4 dark _____

Down

1 write _____

2 day _____

3 low _____

Irregularly Spelled Words

Name: _____ **Date:** _____

Directions: Read each word. Circle the picture that rhymes with the word.

1. own

2. where

3. knew

4. many

5. through

 2

Irregularly Spelled Words

Name: _____ **Date:** _____

Directions: Circle the word with the correct spelling to complete the sentence. Write the word on the line.

1. Kim _____ not want to play

   duz   (does)   dose

2. My teacher is _____ kind.

   very   verry   vere

3. I _____ my mom would like a hug.

   thot   thogt   thought

4. Play that song _____.

   again   agan   agen

5. Turn the lights _____.

   of   off   oof

Irregularly Spelled Words

Name: _____ **Date:** _____

Directions: Read the sentence. Fill in the bubble with the correct word. Write the correct word on the line.

1. Eat dinner _____ you eat dessert.	● before ○ befor
2. I got dessert _____ I ate my dinner.	○ because ○ becuz
3. I want _____ ice cream and cake.	○ both ○ bothe
4. The ice cream was _____.	○ coold ○ cold
5. Mom gave me just the _____ amount.	○ right ○ rite
6. My brother and sister _____ want some, too.	○ allways ○ always

Irregularly Spelled Words

Name: _____**Date:** _____

Directions: Circle the words that have the same vowel sound as the picture.

1.		(off) bone talk
2.		another come son
3.		dirt tub person
4.		hop push could
5.		tip fir pretty
6.		out mop mow

©Shell Education

Irregularly Spelled Words

Name: _____ **Date:** _____

Directions: Write each word in the correct row.

Word Bank

they   buy   my   ~~see~~   weigh   me

rhymes with *bee*	see _____ _____
rhymes with *tie*	_____ _____
rhymes with *hay*	_____ _____

Mixed Review

Name: _____ **Date:** _____

Directions: Circle the word that rhymes with the word in the first box.

1. go	(show)	dog
2. night	mitt	kite
3. buy	big	try
4. eight	late	hat
5. high	fry	fine
6. slow	do	so

Mixed Review

Name: _____ **Date:** _____

Directions: Read each sentence. Fill in the bubble for the sentence that matches the picture.

1. again		● She wants to draw again. ○ Dad will go on the ride again.
2. are		○ They are drinking water. ○ We are having a party.
3. enough		○ Five apples is enough to eat. ○ That is enough fruit.
4. father		○ Father is reading a book. ○ Give the book to father.
5. give		○ The man can give a high five. ○ Sofia will give the dog a bath.

Mixed Review

Name: _____ **Date:** _____

Directions: Draw a picture to match each sentence.

1. Mom is pulling many weeds.	2. Dad will work on the car.
3. Matt will sleep in the tent.	4. Which cereal do you like?
5. Kate read those five books.	6. Dan found nine peas on his plate.

Mixed Review

Name: _____ **Date:** _____

Directions: Read each sentence. Fill in the bubble to show if it is real or make-believe.

1. Some dogs can do tricks.	● real ○ make-believe
2. A duck could have five legs.	○ real ○ make-believe
3. Snow is not cold.	○ real ○ make-believe
4. Both dogs and cats can be pets.	○ real ○ make-believe
5. Green is a color.	○ real ○ make-believe
6. Most pigs have pants.	○ real ○ make-believe

References Cited

Chall, Jeanne S. 1995. *Learning to read: The great debate*, 3rd ed. Orlando: Harcourt Brace.

Cook, Vivian. 2004. *Accomodating brocolli in the cemetary: Or, why can't anybody spell?* New York: Touchstone.

Fry, Edward B., and Jacqueline E. Kress. 2006. *The reading teacher's book of lists*, 5th ed. San Francisco: Jossey-Bass.

Griffith, Priscilla L., and Mary W. Olson. 1992. Phonemic awareness helps beginning readers break the code. *The Reading Teacher*, 45: 516–523.

Juel, C. 1988. Learning to read and write: A longitudinal study of 54 children from first to fourth grades. *Journal of Educational Psychology*, 78: 243–255.

Lomax, Richels G., and Lomax M. McGee. 1987. Young children's concepts about print and meaning: Toward a model of reading acquisition. *Reading Research Quarterly*, 22: 237–256.

National Governors Association Center for Best Practices and Council of Chief State School Officers. 2010. Common core standards. http://corestandards.org/the-standards.

National Reading Panel. 2000. *Report of the National Reading Panel: Teaching children to read*. Washington, DC: Donald N. Langenberg, chair.

Tunmer, William E., and Richard A. Nesdale. 1985. Phonemic segmentation skill and beginning reading. *Journal of Educational Psychology*, 77: 417–427.

page 11
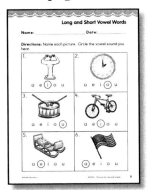

page 15
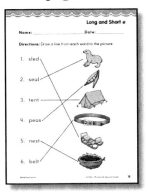

page 19
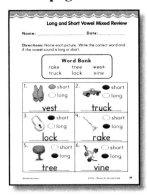

page 12
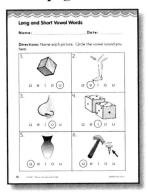

page 16
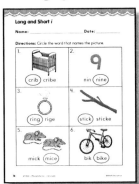

page 20
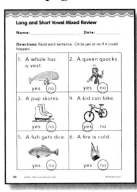

page 13

page 17
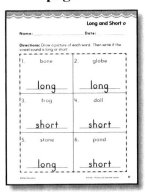

page 21
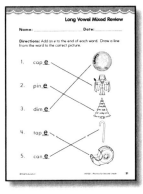

page 14
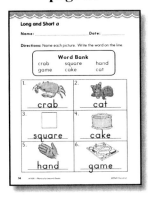

page 18
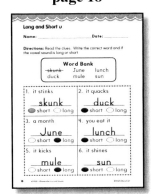

page 22
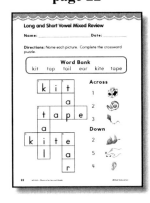

Answer Key (cont.)

page 23

page 27
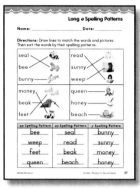

page 31

page 24
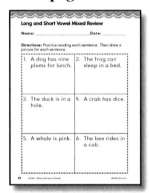

page 28
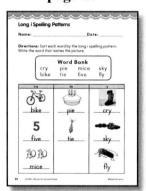

page 32

page 25

page 29

page 33
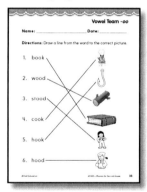

page 26

page 30

page 34

page 35

page 39
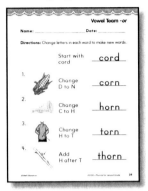

page 43
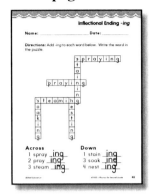

page 36
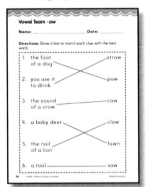

page 40
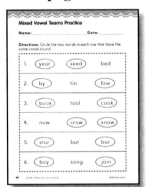

page 44
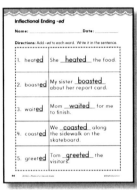

page 37

page 41

page 45

page 38
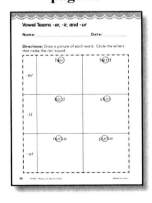

page 42

page 46
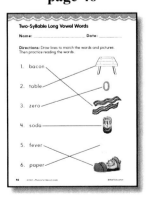

Answer Key *(cont.)*

page 47

Two-Syllable Long Vowel Words

Name: _____ Date: _____

Directions: Write the word for each animal on the line. Practice reading the words.

Word Bank

spider   zebra   eagle
beetle   beaver   ~~tiger~~

1. tiger
2. eagle
3. spider
4. beaver
5. beetle
6. zebra

page 51

Compound Words

Name: _____ Date: _____

Directions: Write the compound word that is the answer. Then practice reading the words.

1. A **boat** with a **sail** is a
   sailboat
2. A **ball** made of **snow** is a
   snowball
3. A **plane** that flies in the **air** is an
   airplane
4. A **box** for your **mail** is a
   mailbox
5. A **cup** you use for **tea** is a
   teacup
6. The **time** you go to **bed** is your
   bedtime

page 55

Prefix un-

Name: _____ Date: _____

Directions: Add un- to each base word to make a new word. Write the new word on the line to complete the sentence.

un- = not

1. happy — The dog looks unhappy
2. buckle — Unbuckle the seatbelt when you arrive at home.
3. equal — Three and ten are unequal
4. lock — Dad has to unlock the car doors.
5. tie — Please untie your shoes before taking them off.

page 48

Compound Words

Name: _____ Date: _____

Directions: Write a compound word to match each picture. Then practice reading the compound words.

Word Bank

man- air bow box tea shell
mail rain sea plane fire- cup

1. fireman
2. airplane
3. mailbox
4. seashell
5. teacup
6. rainbow

page 52

Prefix re-

Name: _____ Date: _____

Directions: Circle the prefix re- in each word. Then write the base word.

re- = to do again

1. recheck — check
2. rename — name
3. replay — play
4. rewrite — write
5. redo — do
6. retry — try

page 56

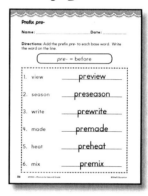

Prefix pre-

Name: _____ Date: _____

Directions: Add the prefix pre- to each base word. Write the word on the line.

pre- = before

1. view — preview
2. season — preseason
3. write — prewrite
4. made — premade
5. heat — preheat
6. mix — premix

page 49

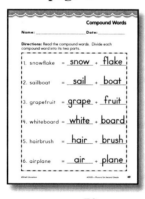

Compound Words

Name: _____ Date: _____

Directions: Read the compound words. Divide each compound word into its two parts.

1. snowflake = snow + flake
2. sailboat = sail + boat
3. grapefruit = grape + fruit
4. whiteboard = white + board
5. hairbrush = hair + brush
6. airplane = air + plane

page 53

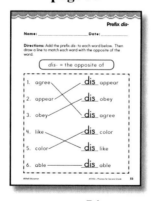

Prefix dis-

Name: _____ Date: _____

Directions: Add the prefix dis- to each word below. Then draw a line to match each word with the opposite of the word.

dis- = the opposite of

1. agree — dis appear
2. appear — dis obey
3. obey — dis agree
4. like — dis color
5. color — dis like
6. able — dis able

page 57

Suffixes -er and -est

Name: _____ Date: _____

Directions: Add -er and -est to each base word. Then practice reading the new words.

-er = more   -est = most

	-er	-est
1. fast	faster	fastest
2. smart	smarter	smartest
3. deep	deeper	deepest
4. rich	richer	richest
5. slow	slower	slowest
6. tall	taller	tallest

page 50

Compound Words

Name: _____ Date: _____

Directions: Write each compound word in the correct row.

Word Bank

butterfly   ~~grapefruit~~   spaceman
goldfish   strawberry   fireman

Fruits	grapefruit / strawberry
Animals	butterfly / goldfish
Jobs	spaceman / fireman

page 54

Prefix over-

Name: _____ Date: _____

Directions: Add the prefix over- to the base words below. Then practice reading the words.

over- = too much

1. grown — overgrown
2. cook — overcook
3. do — overdo
4. mix — overmix
5. eat — overeat
6. study — overstudy

page 58

Suffix -er

Name: _____ Date: _____

Directions: Name each picture. Add -er to the base word in the Word Bank. Write it on the line.

-er = one who

Word Bank

read   farm   ~~teach~~   paint

1. teacher
2. farmer
3. painter
4. reader

page 59

page 63

page 67

page 60

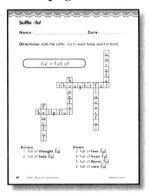

page 64

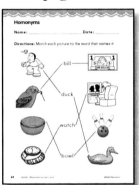

page 68

page 61

page 65

page 69

page 62

page 66

page 70

Answer Key (cont.)

page 71

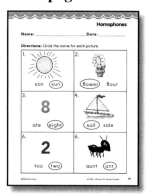

page 72

page 73

page 74

page 75

page 76

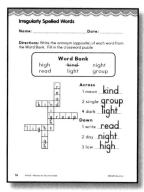

page 77

page 78

page 79

page 80

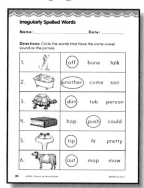

page 81

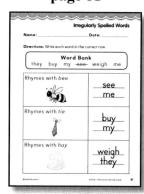

page 82

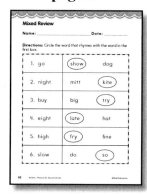

page 83

page 84

page 85

Contents of the Digital Resource CD

Page	Filename	Page	Filename
11	page11.pdf	50	page50.pdf
12	page12.pdf	51	page51.pdf
13	page13.pdf	52	page52.pdf
14	page14.pdf	53	page53.pdf
15	page15.pdf	54	page54.pdf
16	page16.pdf	55	page55.pdf
17	page17.pdf	56	page56.pdf
18	page18.pdf	57	page57.pdf
19	page19.pdf	58	page58.pdf
20	page20.pdf	59	page59.pdf
21	page21.pdf	60	page60.pdf
22	page22.pdf	61	page61.pdf
23	page23.pdf	62	page62.pdf
24	page24.pdf	63	page63.pdf
25	page25.pdf	64	page64.pdf
26	page26.pdf	65	page65.pdf
27	page27.pdf	66	page66.pdf
28	page28.pdf	67	page67.pdf
29	page29.pdf	68	page68.pdf
30	page30.pdf	69	page69.pdf
31	page31.pdf	70	page70.pdf
32	page32.pdf	71	page71.pdf
33	page33.pdf	72	page72.pdf
34	page34.pdf	73	page73.pdf
35	page35.pdf	74	page74.pdf
36	page36.pdf	75	page75.pdf
37	page37.pdf	76	page76.pdf
38	page38.pdf	77	page77.pdf
39	page39.pdf	78	page78.pdf
40	page40.pdf	79	page79.pdf
41	page41.pdf	80	page80.pdf
42	page42.pdf	81	page81.pdf
43	page43.pdf	82	page82.pdf
44	page44.pdf	83	page83.pdf
45	page45.pdf	84	page84.pdf
46	page46.pdf	85	page85.pdf
47	page47.pdf		
48	page48.pdf		
49	page49.pdf		

Notes

Notes